"You'r~ ~~~ ~~~~~,

You're Not Good-Lookin,

You Better Work Hard"

Memorable, Funny

Stories and Life Lessons

from One of America's

Unknown Successes

By

Jack Furlong

Copyright Page

Contents

Copyright Page...................................... ii

Introduction.. 1

First Business Venture............................. 4

The Trap.. 6

The Art of Boxing 8

Down-To-Earth 10

You Win Some and You Lose Some 11

Flying Solo... 13

Sixteen Tons.. 14

Trixie.. 16

Branded 17

Vanilla Extract..................................... 19

Being Men... 20

Testing... 21

The Turnip.. 22

In Honor of Mae West................................ 23

Billy... 24

A Self-Taught Man 26

Big George 27

George Encil Furlong 28

United Mine Workers 31

Typing Lessons 32

Working in the Mines 33

The Thief 36

Life as a Marine 37

The Wild Ride 41

Lois 44

Dinner is Served 47

Caught Between Two Dishes 49

Do You Have Insurance? 50

Insanity Plea 52

Benton Brawlers 53

Tales of Mexico 57

The Tarahumara Indians 81

Ailee Kenboom 84

John Weidman 87

Africa 97

Egypt and Israel 103

Moldova 107

Greece 111

Ireland 112

Germany..113

Austria...116

Introduction

We live in a beautiful, strange, and often funny world. If you stop and think about your life experiences and your life stories, you would probably be amazed at how much you have experienced and how much you really have been blessed.

After retiring from a very successful business career, my father decided to write down some of his most memorable life stories. He has always been a good story teller and has loved sharing these stories with friends and family throughout the years. Some of these accounts all in our family have heard many times, but I have to admit, as I read through this book, many were new to me.

The title, *You're Not Smart, You're Not Good-looking, You Better Work Hard* came from some typical words of wisdom from my grandfather to my dad. Those were not the days of "You're special/feel good about yourself" but rather "Shoot it straight, no feeling sorry for yourself, the world doesn't owe you anything" times. Dad has often quoted those words, has taken them to heart, and has built a great life.

When I read some of these tales I shook my head and wondered, "What were they thinking? Who does that?" However, none of these are made up; they are all true. Some are encouraging, others are strange, and still others simply shed light on the way

1

people and our world work.

Neither my mom nor my dad has ever been those who have sought out the spotlight but wherever they have been, they have always gotten involved, served, and helped make things better. As I thought about the stories shared here, I realized afresh what an impact they have had on the lives of many, many people.

Not only did they build very prosperous lives financially, despite coming from poor coal-mining and farming families, but through their involvement in all types of missionary activities they have impacted thousands and thousands of lives. Simply because they were willing to take action and do something to improve the world, orphanages, schools, churches, and more have been built and continue to serve people years later.

In this book, dad shares stories of growing up in a different time with some pretty crazy adventures. He talks about life in the Marines and how learning a skill in high school may have saved his life. He shares stories about business and family life and some of the wacky things that happen while simply doing your best.

Then you hear about places and people in several parts of Mexico that most Americans never new existed. You get short, but insightful, descriptions of their way of thinking and their customs: normal to them but strange to those outside their world. He then goes on to Africa and shares even more unique perspectives and practices that make you realize our way is not the only way and that it is really nice to live in America.

Reading these stories I came away with a few lasting thoughts:

- My dad has lived quite a life
- This world is beautiful and strange
- God can use anyone if they are simply willing to step out, trust Him, and try

I hope you see those same lessons and quite a few more as you read my dad's funny and unusual stories.

Mark Furlong, 2015

First Business Venture

I was born July, 1931. WWII started December 7, 1941. I remember hearing President Roosevelt saying this was a day of Infamy, and war was declared.

Immediately, Rich and I declared our own war on the dirty Nazi's and those cowardly Japanese. Naturally, we were ready to defend our hometown.

This is when I tried my first business venture. Rich and I swiped a keg of railroad spikes (this was easy as the railroads hauled the coal away every day) that had been mined, and they were always repairing the tracks. Every day at the close of the first shift at the mines, the steam engines would haul the coal away. We called them the "Mile Long Drags." The engines would start very slowly, pulling many loaded coal cars away. Rich and I took a look, and the coal cars had two wheels in front and, a long distance later, the rear wheels would come along. We sat by the tracks and placed a railroad spike on the tracks and waited for the rail wheels to flatten them. The next car would come along and we would repeat the process. We were going to sell the flattened spikes to other kids for three cents each. After all, this was pure profit as we had no overhead. Production was coming along pretty well but we were about out of spikes, when Earl Duncan, Rich's father, came along. He was walking along the tracks, going home from working in the mines. He spotted two young businessmen, in full production, grabbed each of them by the shirt collars and pulled us away. He then put us in front of him, and every step would kick first Rich, then me. We were literally kicked out of our first business venture.

We did make a net profit. We sold the flattened spikes to other kids, as bayonets, so we could defend our country.

We made the country safe; there were no German or Japanese soldiers within our range.

The Trap

I am a depression baby. Dad was a coal miner. He did not work on a regular shift and, during the summertime, hardly at all. The miners received, as part of their compensation, coal. We heated our house with coal. Mom cooked all our meals on a coal-fired stove in the kitchen. So coal was an expensive commodity.

Someone was stealing the coal from our basement. The coal was unloaded into the basement from a coal chute on the side of the house. The house also had a rear-entry try door from the back of the house into the basement.

As only two boys with vivid imaginations could, we decided to set a trap for the thief and show our father we could take care of things. So we set the trap and went to bed. Sometime in the middle of the night there was a loud noise and much yelling. Bob woke me up and said, "Wake up, Jack. We caught the thief." We quickly went to the basement. Much to our surprise, we had captured our father. He had worked the second shift and decided to check the furnace in the basement to be sure the fire didn't go out.

You can imagine our surprise. Our trap had worked to perfection. The bucket of water over the door gave dad a cold shower in the middle of winter. The wires and ropes we had set up had Dad so snared and tangled that it took us several minutes to set a rather irate father free.

I won't discuss the repercussions as a result of our trap.

The Art of Boxing

There were always some boxing gloves around the house when I was growing up. We boys would put the gloves on and flail away at each other. We were not good, but we enjoyed ourselves.

When I started high school, WWII was still going on. Boxing was a requirement in PE class. Early on, the coach would pick out two boys of the same weight and put them in the ring. It was the beginning of an elimination tournament. Early on, he picked Billy Berckle and Charlie Scanavanio. They were the same weight. Charlie was very short and rather pudgy, with a smile for everyone. Charlie was not an athlete. Billy was rather tall, very thin, very reserved, and shy. The coach rang the bell. Charlie came charging across, his arms swinging like windmills. Billy stuck his left hand out, stuck it in Charlie's nose, and started backing up. There was not one blow struck. Charlie's arms were flailing, and Billy started backing up. The coach stopped the bout after one round, he was laughing so hard. He mercifully disqualified both of them.

I won a couple of bouts and started feeling pretty cocky about myself. One day, at home, I asked Dad to spar with me a little. I wanted to show Dad how good I was. Dad replied, "No, son. I'll hurt you." I said, "These are 16oz gloves. They're like pillows. You won't hurt me." I suppose Dad wanted to bring me down a little. We put the gloves on. I jabbed out with my left to feel him out. He flicked my hand aside and hit me three times with his left. It felt like a mule kicking me in the face. It had the desired effect from Dad. I immediately lost interest in the Manly Art of Boxing.

Down-To-Earth

One day, I was about 18 years of age and day-dreaming. I told Dad if I had certain things, I would do wonders. Dad quickly brought me back to earth. He said, "Jack, you're not rich and you're sure as hell not good looking. You had better make up your mind you're going to have to work for a living."

You Win Some and You Lose Some

As I have said, we lived in a small coal mining town. Across the street from us lived the Duncan family. There were four boys: Bill (two years older than me), Richard (my age), Jim (two years younger than me), and Jack (some four years older than me).

Richard and I seemed to have the same interests and other ways of getting into mischief.

This was the depression era. Richard and I went down the alleys looking for soda and milk bottles that had been thrown away. We could get anywhere from a penny to two pennies, depending on the brand of soda or milk bottles we could find. If we came across a plain milk bottle with no brand, we could get as much as a nickel for it. This was the deposit the retailers would charge for the bottles.

After we built up our kitty, we went into the back room of Pete's Pool Room and Pub. Pete had a slot machine in the back. They were illegal, but Pete had one. Richard and I would get a box, deposit our nickel, and play the slot. One day, magic hit. We hit the jackpot. The nickels started rolling out. Rich and I took our ball caps to catch the nickels. I didn't know there were that many nickels in the world.

After the machine quit spitting out those wonderful coins, we were in awe. Then it dawned on us: if we were caught with all those nickels, how could we explain to our parents all this wealth? We decided to try to spend it all. We went to the local malt shop and bought ourselves a giant milkshake. Then we went to get a real hamburger, all our own. Our parents never knew of our having spent so much money.

Flying Solo

Rich and I had been to the movies and saw a film about the daring young men who had experimented making aircraft and how they developed airplanes that were helping the United States win the war.

We decided to build our own airplane. We managed to get a couple of wooden orange crates from the back of a grocery store and started our design and construction. The finished product had an orange crate for the fuselage. We had dismantled some and made the wings. We found an old inner-tube someone had thrown away. It was to be our propulsion. Finally, we made a wooden propeller. It took a lot of work but we finally got the plane up on top of the Duncan's garage at the back of the house. I volunteered to be the test pilot. Rich wound the inner-tube full power. Just as I said, "Contact and ready to take off," Mrs. Duncan came out the back door just in time to see my heroic take off. She yelled, "Good God, no!" By that time, Rich had given me a shove, and the propeller was working beautifully. I moved forward. Sad to say, I went down much quicker than I had moved forward. I crash landed rather quickly.

Mrs. Duncan came over to be sure I had survived then, for some reason, she seemed to get rather angry.

That ended my flying career.

Sixteen Tons

There was a country singer, Tennessee Ernie Ford, who had a major hit song titled "Sixteen Tons." For my generation and older ones, that song had true meaning.

The major employers in our area were the coal mines. My father and virtually all of my friends' fathers were coal miners.

The coal companies would sink the shaft and start the mining operations. They would build small homes around the mine operation; the miners virtually lived on the job site. The company would open a general store, selling basic clothing and food supplies.

The wives would go to the company store to buy their needs. They would charge their purchases to her husband's account. When pay day would come around, whatever had been charged against his account would be deducted. With coal being used to heat the homes and to cook with and the groceries and clothing being purchased through the company store, it was not unusual for the miner to actually owe more than his pay amounted to. It was almost impossible to get ahead under these circumstances. This is one reason the miner's union got started.

The starting line in the song said, "You load sixteen tons and what do you get? Another day older and deeper in debt." To people of my generation and older ones than Lois and me, that song had true meaning.

Trixie

When we lived in Kincaid, my older brother Eldon (Bob) had picked up a small dog and named her Trixie. This dog was Bob's pet.

Every night, we would go through this routine. Bob and I shared the bed. We would go to bed. Mom would call out, "Bob, do you have that dog in bed with you?" Bob would say, "No, Mom. She is on the floor." As soon as he had told Mom the dog was on the floor, he would then say, "Come on, Trixie! Hop up in the bed with us."

This was our routine. One night, I rolled over and Trixie bit my foot. I started crying and Bob immediately tried to get me to shut up. It was too late; both Mom and Dad came into the bedroom to see what was wrong, why was I crying. Mom pulled the covers back. There lay Trixie along with six pups. She had given birth, and I had kicked one of the pups, which was why she had bit me.

Needless to say, Bob and I paid the price for not being totally truthful when it came to the dog sleeping in bed with us.

Branded

My earliest memories: we lived in a small coal mining town called Kincaid, Illinois. My father was a coal miner. The home we lived in was heated by a coal stove in the corner of the living room. In fact, in those days, the miner received coal as part of his pay.

The stove was a large black stove, as I said, coal-fired. The stove had a chrome-looking grill around the lower portion of it. The grill had the flower of daisies and the words "Morning Glory" above and below the flowers: Morning on top and Glory on the bottom. I was about seven or eight years of age. Mom had given me a bath. I ran from the bathroom to stand in the nice warm corner to put my Long-John underwear on. My younger brother Earl, who was between three and four years of age, came over and bit me on the stomach. I instinctively backed up and backed into the grill of a very hot stove. I was instantly branded on my left buttock. I had a nice daisy flower and the words "Morning Glory" above and below the flower.

The brand did not fade away until my sophomore year in high school. You can image the looks and teasing I received. I was the kid with a flower on his butt.

PE class and shower after PE was an interesting time.

When I use the word bathroom, we had no indoor plumbing

at the time. The bathroom was where Mom chose to set the large, round, metal washtub. Usually, it was in the corner of the kitchen. The toilet was an outhouse at the back of the lot.

In fact, on Halloween, the larger boys thought it was a great trick to go down the alleys and turn the outhouses over.

Vanilla Extract

The only time I was ever drunk in my lifetime it was on vanilla extract.

Bob and I were in the kitchen. One of us picked up this bottle of vanilla and said, "I dare you to drink this!" The reply was, "I will if you will!" whereupon both of us drank quite a bit of the extract. The result of this was we both were plastered. Bob tried to get something out of the top shelf of the cupboard. We did not have built in kitchen cabinets. As he climbed up the cupboard, he slipped and pulled the entire cupboard on top of him. All of mom's dishes were in the cupboard. Here was Bob laying on the floor and the cupboard on top of him. Obviously, I was going to help my brother, so I climbed up on the cupboard which was lying on top of Bob as he was on the floor. I started saying, "Don't worry, Bob. I'll get you out." Bob immediately replied, "You idiot! You're standing in the cabinet. How can you help me get out when you're standing on me?"

There were some severe punishments meted out after we sobered up.

Being Men

When Bob and I started to realize we were going to be men someday, we decided to sneak in, get Dad's razor, and do some shaving, although we had no whiskers. It is always best to know what to do when the time arrives.

We were getting near Christmas, and Santa Claus was going to be on the radio. The closest radio station was in Taylorville. The big day arrived. We were gathered around the radio and much to our dismay, the first words out of the mouth of Santa was, "If two boys named Bob and Jack don't quit playing with their Dad's razor, they are not going to get a thing for Christmas." I was panic-stricken. Bob jumped up and yelled, "Who squealed?"

We'll never know if our parents sent the note to Santa or he just made something up out of thin air, but it sure hit home and struck panic in two boys' hearts.

Testing

One time, Richard Duncan, the neighborhood boy, and I had been exploring the woods, creeks, and having a great time pretending we were real frontiersmen.

I missed supper and came home late. Mom prepared a plate of food for me. I was sitting at the kitchen table when Earl, my younger brother, picked up my genuine Red Ryder BB gun, walked over to Dad, and asked Dad to cock it for him. Dad did and loaded the gun. Earl promptly comes over to where I was eating my supper. He put the barrel up against my back and pulled the trigger. Needless to say, I reacted immediately. Mom asked Early why he did that after things had calmed down a little and Earl, with his cool logical way, says, "I wanted to see if it would go through."

The Turnip

Our older sister Maxine could get rather emotional from time to time. Her birthday was the last of October. Mom went to a great deal of trouble to make this a special day for Maxine. She prepared all of my sister's favorite food (fried chicken) and a lot of other things. Supper was just about ready to put on the table. Mom had all of the food on an area on the stove. Bob and I were outside roughhousing as usual. One of us, I don't remember which one, picked up a frozen turnip we found in the back yard and threw the turnip at the other. The turnip took off like a Frisbee, sailed overhead, right into the kitchen window, breaking the glass, and landed right in the middle of a platter of fried chicken; the rest of the glass settled onto the rest of all of Maxine's favorite foods.

Needless to say, we did not have a celebration of my sister's favorite foods. We had bologna sandwiches, Maxine got all emotional and cried, Bob and I were headed northwards, and we got our south ends tanned pretty good.

Such was a normal day in the Furlong household.

In Honor of Mae West

The "D" family lived across the street from us. Mr. "D" worked in the coal mine. He was always very nice, but he had a weakness for alcohol.

He would receive his pay and then hit the bars. As evening approached his oldest son, would come over. We would walk to the taverns in town looking for his father. We would usually find him in a back alley. His son would roll his drunken father of any money he had left and then take the money home to his mother.

One day, Mr. "D" was home by himself. He saw me, called me over to his house, and said, "Jack, how would you like to earn fifty cents?" That was a world of money to me. I said, "Yes." Mr. "D" said, "Go get a match and set my house on fire on the west side in honor of Mae West." I ran to our home and into the kitchen as fast as I could looking for some matches. My mother saw me and wanted to know what I was going to do with the matches. I told her it was in honor of Mae West; Mr. "D" was going to pay me. Needless to say, my mother stopped me from earning a much coveted fifty cents.

Billy

When I was about 11 or 12 years of age, Bob and I somehow managed to get a baby goat. It was a male. Naturally, we named him Billy. Since male goats naturally seem to want to butt things, it wasn't hard for Bob and me to teach him to butt. We would get down on our knees and put our heads against him and push. Billy got the idea very quickly. We had a good time getting Billy to give our friends a push or two when they would come over to our home.

One day, in the fall, Bob and I were in school. When we arrived home, we had one very angry mother. It seems while we were at school, Mom did the laundry. There were no clothes dryers in those days. While she was in the backyard hanging the damp clothes on the clothesline, Mom was bent over getting some clothing out of her basket. Billy saw an inviting target and gave our mother an unexpected push. He hit her with a full force blow in her rear end and sent our mother headfirst into a basket of wet clothes.

Needless to say, when we got home from school, we met one irate mother. We were informed Billy was a persona non grata and he was to leave our premises that day.

My brother Bob told Mom he would take Billy away that evening as he was going to the first high school basketball game of the season. Bob left with the goat. Later, I walked the two miles into town to Johnston City to watch the game. As one entered the gym, there were two doors with a metal railing separating the doors. After the game was over and the crowd was leaving, suddenly there was some excitement at the exit door. It seems as if Bob had tied Billy to the railing and as people were leaving the gym, they had to pass by Billy. Billy was rather excited and seemed to be butting anyone he could as they left the gym. Needless to say, he was the center of attention. I walked on by and never acknowledged that was my goat.

There was an Italian immigrant farmer nearby that had a flock of goats. He sold goat milk and cheese, and he was very happy to give Billy a good home.

A Self-Taught Man

My father was a large man: 6' 2", about 240 lbs. He had a 3rd grade education. He went to work in the coal mines at the age of 12, shovelling coal for the rate of a dime a ton of coal he shovelled into a car. He was blue collar and felt if anyone wore a white shirt and a tie to work, they were successful. He, himself, was self-taught. I remember as a child, he would work his shift in the coal mines and then at night would go back to the mines to work for free to learn the skills of the man who had a job above his so when an opening occurred, he would have a chance for the job. As a result, over the years, he passed the exams in the State of Illinois as a safety examiner, hoisting engineer, mine manager, and mine superintendent.

Big George

As a young man of about sixteen or seventeen, the carnivals would come through the small coal mining towns and anyone who could last three rounds with the fighter, he would receive $50. Dad was the fighter who took on all comers. Needless to say, he was known as Big George in the local area.

George Encil Furlong

George Encil Furlong was the youngest of Franklin Furlong and Sarah Shaw Furlong. He had two older brothers: Ralph and Ellis and a sister: Lena. His parents divorced when he was an infant and he never knew his father. After the divorce, his mother ran a boarding house and took in washings and other menial chores to support her family. When George was twelve years old, he went to work in the coal mines in southern Illinois. The pay that he received was ten cents for each ton of coal he shovelled. His mother would then take his pay and would tell him that it was to help support the family. When George was 17, he was about 6 feet 2 inches tall and weighed 220 pounds. He was known as "Big George" in the coal mines. He married Tressie Pearl Joplin when he was 18 and she was 19. They had eight children: Lena Maxine, Eldon Laverne, Jack Daniel, Earl Lee, Jerry Encil, Jeanne Sharon, and Pamela. When they were married, George worked in the coal mines. Before the birth of their child, he secured work in Akron, Ohio working in a rubber factory making tires. When working in Ohio, he became ill and had to have an appendectomy. He missed several days of work due to the surgery and because of this, he lost his job. He then decided to return to southern Illinois where he worked for a short time on the farm for Daniel and Loral. In the mid-1930s, new coal mines were being opened in central Illinois and for this reason, George and Tressie moved to Kincaid, Illinois. While he was here, he was able to find a job. George was a proud and ambitious man who would often work his shift during the day and return to the mines to work at night for no pay. He did this in order to learn the skills for the job which gave higher pay. This gave him an advantage over others because when an opening occurred, he had the skills necessary to perform in this position. He studied and passed the State of Illinois exams for safety, engineer, hoisting engineer, mine manager, and mine superintendent. In his last years working in the mines, he was a face boss and had a crew of miners working under him. In 1953, the mine he worked in closed and he found himself out of a job. He went to Jacksonville, Illinois and secured employment as a fireman's helper in a state mental hospital. The hospital operated their own power plant for heat and electricity. He immediately started to learn what the firemen's obligations were and soon had a fireman's position. He then began to study for the operating engineer's position and within four years, he had passed the State of Illinois Boards as an operating engineer. This is the position which he held until his retirement. He was a staunch union man and was one of the original members of the United Mine Workers of America which was involved with the labor troubles in the 1930s which strived to get benefits for workers. When he went to work for the state of Illinois, he immediately joined the union. For several years, he was the president of the local Brotherhood of Operating Engineers. He was constantly being requested for assistance in getting jobs for various people. He took great satisfaction in being able to help in this manner. He came to know many important politicians during this time and because of this, he was offered a position with the international union. Because he did not want to get involved with the travel, he turned down the position. He retired from his job as an operating engineer and lived in Jacksonville, Illinois until his death. He was a quite person with a wry sense of humor. He was a proud man who often stated that the only helping hands a man could expect were at the end of his arms. He was proud of the fact that even during the depression, he never once asked for aid, relief, or assistance and that he stood on his own two feet to support his family. He was honest with great integrity. He once told me, "Jack, there are two kinds of bones: wishbones and backbones. Which kinds do you have?" He felt a man's word and reputation were the only things of true value a man could have. He often stated, "It is easy to make a mistake but regardless of how good the treasure, there is still a blot on the paper. The best thing is to be honest and forthright in your dealing." About three years before his death, he became a Christian and began attending church services with Tressie. Dad once made a comment to me: "Jack, you're not rich and you're sure as hell not good looking so you might as well make up your mind you're going to have to work for a living." It was good advice; one which I have tried to follow.

United Mine Workers

I remember when the unions were trying to get organized with the miners, Dad immediately joined. He was one of the original members of the United Mine Workers. He would go to work with his lunch bucket in one hand and a shot gun in his other. Mom would stand at the door crying, not knowing if he would come home on a slab or upright.

Typing Lessons

My freshman year of high school, I came home after signing up for my classes. Dad asked if I had signed up for typing. I replied no, I had not. He stated, "You will." I replied, "I'll be the only boy taking typing!" Dad said, "Do you want to face your buddies or face me?" I said, "I'll take typing." As a result, I took four years of typing; many times, I was the only boy in typing class.

Working in the Mines

I was going to school in Kentucky when the Korean War started. I came home, went to the local draft board to inquire as to my draft statue, and was informed not to go back to school as my number would be coming up soon.

My father helped me get a job in the coal mines after that. I started as a track layer. My pay was $2.08 per hour, which was good money in 1950. Miners were paid higher wages because of the danger factor.

In 1948, there was a cave in at the mine I worked in. Twenty-eight men were killed.

In December of 1951, at the Orient #2, there was an explosion that killed 119 men. In a small community like ours, it was devastating. I was a pall bearer at three funerals on Christmas Day, 1951. The first man brought out was Herschel Summers. He was cut in half by a flying 2x4 board, more than a mile from the scene of the explosion. The last man brought out was Johnny Chestie. He, too, was a friend of mine. There was one man in that crew found alive.

I went down in the mine. We went more than 600 feet down and worked under a town called Johnston City, six miles from where we went down.

33

I was a track layer. After an area had been mined out, the safety inspector would go in, check for methane gas, and examine the top for loose rock. If the area was deemed safe to work in, two men would check the top and put in six inch oak poles to prop up any soft spots and then my crew would come in and level the floor and put in the tracks so the machines would have a stable base. The next two men came in with the cutting machine. This was a large machine that had a blade like a chainsaw blade laid parallel to the ground. They would cut an area. The blade was about ten feet in length. They would cut a semi-circle cut, about six inches above the base. A man with a long, flat shovel would reach in the cut and shovel out the coal dust. Coal dust was very flammable and could start an explosion. Next came two men with the drilling machine. They would drill several holes about two inches in diameter in the various spots in the face of the coal. Next came Boomer, the shot firer. In my opinion, one had to have a lot of nerve or be crazy to do his job. He would insert hollow steel tubes in the holes which had flanges on them so they would dig into the coal and then blast the coal loose. Then the Joy machine operator would come in. This was a large machine with two large steel rotating arms on them scooping the coal onto a conveyor belt into a coal car to haul the coal out. When the area was cleaned out, they would move on to the next area that had been prepared. The arm going straight ahead was called the face. The sides were called ribs. We would then start on an angle, side rooms and start the process over.

The Thief

I was surprised to see mice down in the mine in areas where we could eat. An old timer told me if you see the mice getting out, you better go with them.

We would take our lunch in a miner's bucket. The bottom was an aluminium pail which would hold about a gallon of water. It was a pail. A lunch container would nest into the top of the pail, which would hold sandwiches, fruit, etc. Above this was a smaller container which could hold cookies, a piece of pie, etc. We would put our buckets in a safe place and when lunch time came, we could eat our lunch. We had a thief in our midst. Someone was coming by and stealing our desserts. Boomer, the shot firer, had his wife make a piece of chocolate pie out of Ex-Lax. The thief ate the chocolate pie and it soon became obvious who the culprit was. At this, Boomer told him what would happen to him if any more dessert was missing. That solved the problem.

Life as a Marine

I received a letter from the local draft board informing me my friends and neighbors had selected me to represent them in the armed forces of the United States. I never have met anyone who identified themselves as to who volunteered me. We loaded onto buses and arrived at the Federal Court house in St. Louis.

We were informed that a certain percentage of us would be sent into the Marines. I later found out the Marines had suffered many casualties in the Chosin Reservoir and needed some bodies in a hurry. After WWII ended, our military was cut back way too much and the United States was not prepared in any way for military action. As a result, in the early stages of the Korean War, the United States suffered some severe beatings and losses. I was one of the ones selected for the Marines. I now feel it was the best for me. There is a saying, "Once a Marine, always a Marine." I found that to be true.

As soon as I was notified I was to be a Marine, we were separated from the rest of the other draftees. I entered a room and was given a packet giving me my travel orders, my serial number, and other goodies. I don't know when I went into the Marines but it was well before I got to the court house in St. Louis.

We were boarded onto a train and left immediately for San

Diego, California for boot camp. After two days on the train, we arrived in San Diego about 1:00 a.m. There were several young men who were Navy Boots also. A couple of Navy Chiefs called out, "All you Navy men! Load on the buses! Let's go!" They left. Then there were three men: two buck Sergeants and a Corporal, they were large physical specimens; they looked like Marines. One of the Sergeants called out, "You Marines! Fall out! Platoon formation! Column of fours! Dress right and cover down!" We were still in the depot in downtown San Diego and had no idea what he was talking about. It wasn't long before we were lined up in four columns and in perfect alignment with the men on our right. Red Morthland was standing chewing gum and looking around. One of the Sergeants came over, slapped Red across the face, and said, "You're at attention." Red doubled up his fist and the Corporal behind him pinned his elbows to his side and said, "No you don't!" One man was so tense he fainted and fell face down on the floor. As we were staring at the buses, a drunk in the depot started to mock us and acted like he was marching. One of the new recruits stepped out of line and knocked the drunk down. The Sergeant in our rear smiled, nodded his head, and we boarded onto the buses.

Training began almost immediately. First, we all had our hair cut to bald status. Uniforms were issued, and basic training began.

After a couple of days, a rather intense physical was given. A couple of men were found not to meet standards and were released. There were seventy-five men in our platoon to begin with; some fifteen were dropped for various reasons.

The training was intense but not something a young man who was in good physical condition could not handle. I graduated with my platoon and was told I could wear the title of Marine. I gained some twenty-five pounds and was in excellent physical shape.

After getting a ten day leave, I reported into Camp Pendleton, California. My orders read for duty beyond the seas, which means Korea. Then a strange twist took over. A Colonial Calvert, the disbursing officer for Camp Del Mar, had some spies in the receiving and casual area where men were sorted to various units for assignments, had some people looking over files and I found myself in Colonel Calvert's office, interviewing me. He looked at my file and said, "Your record shows you can type. Is that true?" I replied, "Yes, sir!" He asked, "How fast?" I replied, "Eighty words a minute." Immediately, he said, "You go to the building, report to the Sergeant in charge of the barracks, get your gear set up, and report to my office." I found myself in the Fiscal accounting office, typing out checks and official fiscal reports to headquarters. My father's insistence on my taking typing saved me from the front lines in Korea. I had no idea my typing skills were such a rare commodity.

The Marines are a proud group of people and have pretty high standards for themselves. One man in our unit was a slob, to put it mildly. He did not bathe very often. The men in his immediate area took care of the problem. They picked him up, stripped him, and took him to the area where men could take their dirty uniforms, place them on a wooden area under the water faucets, get a stiff bristle brush, and scrub their dirty uniforms. This man was put on the wooden wash area and was scrubbed very thoroughly with the stiff bristle brushes. When finished, his skin was a bright pink from the cold water scrubbing. From that point on, he was very much in the cleanliness demanded by the Corps.

The Wild Ride

Lois and I were in Madrid, Spain. We decided to have dinner with some friends.

We had heard of a restaurant called "Botin's." This is an old restaurant. Reportedly, the oven was over 500 years old. Hemingway mentioned this restaurant in his book, *For Whom the Bell Tolls.*

Charley Bowden, his wife Bernie, Jack Prade, Lois, and I decided to go there for our evening meal.

The place was as advertised: a very old masonry building and they told us, indeed, the oven was a brick-lined oven that was over 500 years old.

The meal was delicious and an enjoyable evening for all concerned.

When we decided to leave was when the excitement started. The street in front of the restaurant was a divided street with a well-maintained median separating the two lanes of traffic and trees were planted in the median. It was a very pleasant and picturesque site.

The first cab was a small Seat Car, the Spanish version of a Fiat. The cab could only take three passengers. Charley volunteered to take the first cab with the two ladies, and Jack Prade and I would catch the next cab. The three of them left. After a couple of minutes, we caught the next cab.

When I got in the cab, I told the driver the Melia Castellia Hotel. The driver said, "Si." He put the flag down to start the meter. Then, much to our surprise, the cabby made a left turn, went over the curb, over the median and between some trees, completed his U turn, and started driving like he was in a NASCAR race. Jack Prade and I were bouncing around. The car was a stick shift. Needless to say, we were moving about. Jack Prade started yelling, "He's mad! Let me out of here!" I was trying to tell the driver, "No rapido!" He ignored me and floored the gas again. We came to an intersection. Two men were starting to cross the street. The driver seemed to aim at them. At the last minute, one of the men saw us, grabbed his companion, and pulled him back. I literally saw a foot window high as we sped past him.

We arrived at the hotel and were glad to get out of that car. I was sitting on the steps leading up to the hotel waiting for our friends and my wife to arrive.

After a few minutes, the cab pulled up and the three of them got out. Charley came over to me and said, "You won't believe it. We were going 80 kilometres an hour going through the streets of Madrid." I told him, "Charley, you left before we did. We've been here for five minutes. I have no idea how fast we were going; I was too busy trying to stay upright from being bounced around that car and yelling for the drive to slow down!"

Lois

Lois is my wife.

I first met her July 17, 1949. My best friend Buddy Sims' parents had his 18th birthday party. I attended. Lois and some of her girlfriends from Benton, Illinois' church also attended.

At the time, young people from three towns' (West Frankfort, Benton, and Christopher) church groups would have meetings, play softball, go on hayrides, and do other activities. Each town was about six miles apart; it was a perfect triangle.

My first impression was that Lois was a little bit stuck up. One day, Paul Sullenger, one of my better friends, called and stated he had a date with a girl from Christopher; could I get some wheels and we would go on a double date. I told him I could get the car but see if he could get that red head (stuck up) from Benton to go. The net result: Paul arranged a triple set up. We would go to Christopher, pick up his date and her brother, go to Benton, pick up Joan Smothers, then pick up Lois. Jo Ann was the only one who knew how to get out to Lois' house, out in the country. We would then go to Christopher were we would attend a youth rally at the church there.

I picked Paul up, we went to Christopher, and then the fun began. Paul's date came out but her brother, Francis Hammond, stood on the back porch looking in a mirror trying to get his hair combed just right. After several minutes, I threatened to go without him. That Frances finally got in the car. As we were heading to Benton, the Hammond girl stated she knew where Lois lived. It would save a few minutes. So on her word and direction, I turned off the highway and went down the country road. It soon became obvious she had no idea where Lois lived. She said, "It is a white farmhouse on a hill." They were all white houses. Finally, I saw the name "Tiberend" on a mailbox. That was Lois' last name. I went to the door. A tall man answered. I asked for Lois. He said, "Lois doesn't live here." He asked, "Are you looking for Ed?" I replied I did not know. All I knew was that I had a date with Lois. He gave me directions. By the time we got to Lois' house, she thought she had been stood up, had changed clothes, and was not going anywhere. Her mother convinced her to get dressed. We then went to Benton to get Jo Ann.

Joan was supposed to be the lead singer for the youth program. By the time we got to the church, services had started. Joan went straight up front, sang her songs, and came back to where we were seated. The fun began then. Francis, Joan's date, began shooting spit balls at the speakers up on the Dias. He would hit one and say, "I got one!"

Needless to say, it was embarrassing. As soon as the program was over, Francis jumped up and ran out the door. The rest of us exited, and Francis was up in a tree doing all kinds of stunts. Jo Ann said, "Oh my Lord! That crazy guy is my date." We finally got Francis out of the tree and went to a restaurant. It was supposed to be a nice place. We started to get out of the car, and Francis' sister would not go. She said she would stay in the car. As a compromise, we went to West Frankfort to a drive in. Again, she refused to get out of the car. Paul stayed in the car with her while the rest of us went in to get a hamburger. We could not get the brother and sister back home quick enough. It is a miracle Lois agreed to go out with me again after that.

Dinner is Served

I am a member of the Gideons International. The Gideons had an international convention in St. Louis. Lois and I went to the banquet. I really wanted to hear the principal speaker scheduled that evening. We were seated ten to a table at the banquet. As a waiter passed by our table, he had several plates of food on his tray. Just as he got behind me, a plate slid off his tray and landed on the crown of my head. The plate cracked into two pieces, as if in a movie script, depositing on my head a serving of roast beef, gravy, potatoes, and a generous portion of mixed vegetables. Lois was sitting to my right. She quickly said, "Don't move!" She said, "You have the vegetables on your shoulders," and the gravy was running down my neck. The person in charge came quickly over and attempted to wipe up the gravy with a towel. His beard scratched my ear as he was saying, "I'm sorry. You have food in the chair. Let us bring you a new chair." I agreed. After the meal, I attempted to swing my chair around so I could see the head table and see the guest speaker. I found I could not move. Lois wanted to know what was wrong. I found out the clean chair they brought me had a large wad of pink bubble gum on it. I was stuck in the chair with the gum. I told Lois, "Get your purse. We're going home." I went to the head person and asked, "What have you got against me? I came to the banquet. So far, I have had a plate of food dumped on me and was given a chair filled with bubble gum."

The company did pay for a new suit, as they could not get the gravy stains out of a light grey suit.

My wife was sitting next to me. She had a white dress on. Not one drop of food or gravy had spilled on her. My wife laughed at my dilemma. I don't think I have ever seen her laugh as much as she did that evening.

Caught Between Two Dishes

One Sunday morning, Lois and I were in our pews at church when a couple came in late. The lady was a close friend of Lois'. We moved over to make room for them. I found myself with Lois to my left side, her friend Joy to my right side, and her husband Bob on the outside. I'm between the two ladies. After a few minutes, I took my handkerchief out of my pocket, wiped my brow, and whispered to Lois, "Are you as hot as I am? I'm burning up."

Looking straight ahead, not cracking a smile, she replied, "Your problem is you're sitting between two sexy dishes and picking up the vibrations."

I tried to keep from laughing out loud and literally had my handkerchief over my mouth. Joy leaned over and asked, "What's wrong with you?"

Lois looked straight ahead, as innocent looking as she could be, listening to the sermon.

Do You Have Insurance?

I did insurance investigations for about five years, and I had some interesting experiences. A couple stand out.

I was living in the small southern Illinois town of Vandalia. I was given an assignment.

A man living in the small farm community of Brownstown, Illinois had been to St. Louis to seek employment at McDonald Aircraft Company. He was on his motorcycle going east about 3:00 p.m. in August. A farmer's wife was going west. The sun was directly in her eyes. She made a left turn. She did not see the man on the motorcycle and hit him, knocking him off the road. He was severely injured.

I drew the job of, in essence, doing a lot of work for the attorneys in preparing the defence for the insurance company as the farmer's wife was clearly at fault. I was told to find out what kind of work he did, how much he earned, and as much personal information as I could get. I discovered in the small town he was from that the man was not too well educated. He was an odd job labourer working as a day labor on a farm and working in a saw mill doing odd jobs. But the unusual twist: there was a widow who lived a couple of miles out of town. She had four daughters. This man had lived with each of the four girls at some time. Two of the girls had a child by him. He had married them and later divorced them. At the time of the wreck, he was living with the mother. After the man was released from the hospital, he moved back in with the mother but each of the women took turns caring for him during his recovery.

I violated a company rule and told my wife about the situation. She didn't believe me. When I completed the report, prior to mailing it in, again I violated a company rule and let my wife read it. Her comments: "You mean it is really true?" She had a difficult time believing a situation like this could exist.

Sometimes people are hard to figure out.

Insanity Plea

A local farmer supposedly suddenly became insane and was threatening his wife and anyone else who came on the property. The county Sheriff, Dave, was called. He arrived on the scene. He told the wife, "I know him. We went to school together." He called out and said, "I'm coming to the house to talk to you." The farmer promptly put a bullet into the ground about ten feet in front of the Sheriff. At this point, Dave got behind a large tree in the front yard and instructed a deputy to go to Vandalia and get a tear gas grenade and the grenade launcher. They were going to force the man out of the house with the tear gas. The grenade launcher was delivered. The Sheriff loaded it and fired toward the house. He aimed for a window. He missed the window and hit the side of the house. The grenade bounced off the wall of the house and out into the wheat field. The grenade set the wheat field on fire. At this point, the farmer yelled out, "You idiots! What are you trying to do, burn my wheat crop?" He came running out of the house. He and the sheriff and the deputies worked to put the fire out. Then the farmer was taken to get medical treatment. At least his wheat field was saved.

Benton Brawlers

In February of 1981, Lois and I took a few days off and went to the desert southwest to get away from the winter doldrums and get a little sun. We were in Tucson, Arizona. We decided to look at some real estate in an upscale area to get an idea of the prices in the Tucson area.

We entered an open house. As we entered, we were greeted by the real estate agent who was a man with a very distinct British accent. He introduced himself as Jacque Robilliard. That struck me as odd. I asked how in the world a man with such a French name had such a very British accent. He replied, "When the Normans invaded England a Robilliard was in the Army, and the Robilliards have been in England ever since."

I then asked how he came to the United States, and this is his story.

He stated he was an engineer by education, to be precise a mining engineer. He was an engineering officer in the British army in WWII. Because of his familiarity with the German topographical terrain as he had been in Germany prior to the war as a mining engineer, he was assigned to work with the United States Army engineers on many projects. As a result of his working with the Americans, he became friends with several of them. When the war ended, the Americans returned home. He returned to his old job.

Shortly after the end of the war, an election was held in England, and the Labour party was voted in. One of the first acts of the new Labour government was to nationalize the British mining industry. Since his family owned and operated coal mines, he was informed his services were no longer needed or desired.

Now unemployed, he called some of his American friends and was offered work as a mining engineer in the United States. He was subsequently hired and came to the United States.

Here is when his story struck home with Lois and me.

He stated he was hired and assigned to work in the coal mines. He said he left Chicago, Illinois on a train with the quaint name of the Blue Bird. He arrived in a small town in Southern, Illinois in a town you have never heard of, a town called Benton, Illinois. He arrived late in the evening.

He was given directions to a nearby, rather nondescript hotel, the Benton Hotel, which was close to the train station. He stated he suspected this was a place where ladies of the night plied their trade.

He then stated he became somewhat of a novelty in this small southern Illinois town. He was interviewed and an article was written about him and published in the *Benton Evening News* about the Englishman now living and working in Benton. He became somewhat of a social prize, and he was invited to many people's homes for a meal. He said the people were curious about him and wanted to hear his Limey accent. He felt many of the people in southern Illinois had done very little traveling out of their local area and, except for the many veterans returning from the war, had very little contact with the outside world.

The food was well-prepared, and he remarked about how many beef pot roast dinners he had with mashed potatoes and gravy. He also had scones, which the Americans called biscuits. The wives also served a variety of fruits and vegetables which were grown locally, and many of the wives proudly stated they had canned or made the preserves themselves. If he was not served roast beef, he was served fried chicken.

He was surprised about how little most of the people knew about the outside world and how few of them had done any traveling to any extent. Many people had never met someone from another country, with the exception of the returning soldiers. He stated many of the people had a rather parochial viewpoint.

He then said that a couple of the coal miners took him to a place a few miles out of Benton, a place they called "The Rat Hole." He found it was difficult to describe. He said it certainly could not be called a night club and it was too large to be called a neighborhood pub. The crowd was loud and somewhat rowdy. Suddenly, a fight broke out, and it grew larger. The miners who were with him pushed him under the table. They said, "Limey, you stay here and don't get hurt. This is our time to have some fun." They joined the fray. He stated he considered it a rough brawl. After the fight, the miners took him back to Benton. The miners actually enjoyed the fight and looked forward to going again.

From his description, I think the trip to The Rat Hole shook him up quite a bit.

He stated he was offered employment elsewhere soon after and accepted the job and left Benton.

After he told us his story, Lois and I told him Lois was from Benton and I was from West Frankfort and that both of our fathers were coal miners. At first, he refused to believe us. After a few minutes, we did convince him. We had a rather enjoyable visit with him and then we continued our trip.

It was interesting to see how someone from England viewed our part of the country we called home.

Tales of Mexico

As a result of our frequent trips into Mexico helping build churches, we had some interesting experiences.

With Rich Knickmeyer leading the construction, we assisted a pastor in finishing his church building. Starting in an empty garage it had grown to be a large church. Our team put in electrical, ceiling, and did some drywall work. As the building was nearing completion, Rich and I were standing outside talking to the pastor. I thought nothing could surprise me after all of our experiences, but this one surprised both of us. The pastor calmly says, "Now that we have the temple completed, maybe I should try to find the owner of the ground and offer to pay for it."

When we first started in Mexico, the law stated any building that was used for churches, printing religious material, and meeting purposes was owned by the government. This means any time the government wanted to take over they had the right to do so. Eventually the law was changed, and the church organization could legally own the buildings.

***

We took a team of nineteen men to a place called Yoquivo. It was literally a truly isolated place. We were to build an orphanage for Tarahumara Indian children. The last forty miles took us four hours to drive as there were almost no roads. We were two days from Juarez, the border town. There was a small general store. The only telephone was a solar-powered phone hung on a pole. If there was no sun, there was no phone service. All nineteen of us stayed in a ten foot by twenty foot building. We had our sleeping bags all on the floor. This was truly togetherness. The first thing we built was an outhouse. We showered in the nearby waterfall.

We built the building which was designed to provide for ten boys on one side and ten girls on the other, with a small apartment for the adult couple. It was the only building in the community with indoor plumbing and showers. The first five children to be taken in were all cousins. Their mothers were Tarahumara Indian ladies who were alcoholics with no fathers around. Hector Martinez, a pastor and businessman from Chihuahua City, was to keep watch and supervise the operation.

***

I have had the privilege of visiting several countries. Lois and I became involved in leading teams into the country of Mexico where we assisted in the building of three Bible schools, four elementary schools, a couple of orphanages, a home for abused women, and probably some forty plus churches. As a result of this, we were able to meet some remarkable people. One of these persons was Soledad Marquez, known as Sister Cholla in English and Hermana Cholla in Spanish.

Sister Cholla and another lady went into the city of Juarez where they met a lady who was an invalid. They sat the lady outside of her small home in the sun while they cleaned her home, did her laundry, cooked some food, and then had a little Bible study. The next week, they went back. A couple of the original lady's friends showed up, and the Bible study group grew rapidly. It wasn't long before they outgrew the little home they were meeting in. Then they rented an abandoned chicken coop. They then bought the chicken coop, cleaned it up, and soon they had outgrown the chicken coop. If a child didn't have a dress or a pair of shoes to wear to school, Cholla managed to get the child the shoes or clothes. They then bought a lot of land and started to build a church. The men made the adobe blocks. The ladies would make and sell tortillas, enchiladas, etc., until they had enough money to buy doors, windows, or whatever the need was. They would not go any further until they had paid cash for what was needed for the job. The church building was soon the largest in their area of the city. The area was a slum, extremely poor.

We took a team, did some electrical work, put in a ceiling, and laid the tile. Cholla ordered a pink marble floor tile from

Torrereon, which was noted for the high quality of the floor tile. After our crew had finished a day's work, she would come in and inspect. If she came to a piece of tile that was improperly laid or not the matching color, she would take a hammer, crack the tile, and lay a hammer across the tile. This was her way of saying this did not meet the standards for the House of The Lord. This soon became the largest and most effective church in that area of the city. She never did see herself as a pastor, merely a servant of God, and to help her fellow believers. As time went on, the small children grew to adulthood and became ardent workers in the church. One of these was a young girl, Sandra. She married Jose Rodriguez, and they are pastors of one of the larger churches in the city of Juarez.

Unfortunately, Cholla had a stroke and died in early 2013. I do not know who is leading the congregation now, but she was truly a remarkable servant of Christ. Her name was Soledad Marquez.

***

In Mexico, there is a large canyon called "Barranca de Cobre" (Copper Canyon). It is deeper and larger than the Grand Canyon in Arizona. At the bottom of the canyon is a small village called Botapilas. This is an interesting place. It was literally built by an American. The man was an engineer. In fact, he was the man who designed and laid out the streets in Washington D.C.

He moved to the Copper Canyon and operated a huge silver mine operation. He built the power plant which still provides power to the town. He had a small hospital built, and the silver was melted down into silver bars. When they took the silver out, it was with a well-guarded mule train. He died as a result of a ruptured appendix. There is a small hotel-inn in the town. Lois and I went there. We were taken down in a large four-wheel drive Chevy Suburban. At times, you could look down and see space beneath you but no road; we were that close to the cliff. Halfway down, the driver stopped and cooked some delicious fajitas.

When we arrived, one of the departing guests told us to have Oscar sing for us. He had a beautiful voice. When we got out of our vans, a young man came over and introduced himself as Oscar, the assistant manager. After we were there a couple of days, we went to a small Catholic Church some Jesuit missionaries had built in the 1500 period. In fact, a couple of them are buried in the floor of the church. The church was still in use. About once a month, a priest on his rounds would hold service. To get to the church from the village was interesting. We climbed into the back of a pick-up truck and sat on a car bench someone had thrown in. Needless to say, it was a bumpy ride.

When we arrived at the church, Oscar was there. He asked

what we wanted to hear. He was the singer. We replied he could sing what he wanted. To our amazement, he started to sing. He sang several songs, most with religious themes. He had an opera tenor voice. After he had finished his concert, I went to him and asked what in the world he was doing in such a remote place as Botapilas. He replied, "I am Mexican. In fact, my family lives in Chihuahua City. When I was twelve-years-old, I was sent to Madrid, Spain to study to become a classical pianist." It was there that he started singing. In fact, he had won the Pavarotti opera singing competition in Rome, Italy twice and he was singing in the Metropolitan Opera in New York. He stated the summer times were the slow times in the classical music world. He had seen an ad advertising the need for someone to work at this little inn for the summer. Since his family lived in Chihuahua, he decided to visit his home country, see his family, and pick up a little money in the summer. He was scheduled to be the featured soloist at the Miami, Florida opera that fall.

He gave us a CD with his music and his singing. The following year, Lois and I received an invitation from him inviting us to hear him sing at the Metropolitan Opera in New York. We did not go, but we did get to hear a beautiful tenor down in the bottom of Copper Canyon.

***

Josefina Valenzuela is a person whom you will never forget having met her.

After graduation from the University in Mexico City, she went to the city of Juarez. She started working with small children and, to the other extreme, hardened criminals. She lived in a house where the government had assigned some criminals on parole to her care. Josefina is a tiny lady; I doubt she weighs 100 pounds. She kept a large black dog as her companion at night and in her bedroom. The dog was well-trained. She even had a couple of men assigned to her who had killed a person. She would get the men jobs and try to get them back as useful citizens.

As only Josefina could do, she had some ground given to her at the outside of the city. Her intent was to build an orphanage. After she had clear title of the property in the church's name, we took a team down and built a two-story concrete block building. The building was designed to house twenty-four boys plus house a small apartment for Josefina to live in. Within six months, she had fifty boys in the building. There was a small bodega (warehouse on the property). We took another team down and remodelled the bodega, giving her more space for more boys. During this time, the Juarez police brought two boys to her, seven and nine years of age. They told Josefina these boys had been brutally beaten by their drug addicted parents and, in the opinion of the police, these boys had been damaged beyond help.

We later took another team down and built a building designed to house fifty girls. We also started a building to house a small medical clinic.

When the two boys mentioned earlier took a test, they both scored extremely high academically. In fact, the older one was awarded $1000 for a scholarship when he became college-age. The award was published in the Juarez newspaper. When the authorities read this, they came to the orphanage and took the boys to put them in a proper home, not this little nondescript orphanage. In Mexico, if a child is twelve or over in a living dispute, the child can make the decision to where they want to live. The following day, the boys were returned to the orphanage. The older of the two boys was also an extremely gifted soccer player, and his skills soon became well-known throughout the Juarez area. When he was seventeen years old, a scout for a pro soccer team came to the orphanage to talk to Josefina and the boy. They were told they ranked him in the top ten players in the country of Mexico, ages seventeen to nineteen. The scout told Josefina he was quite concerned about the boy because they worried when he turned pro how would he handle all of the money and fame he would have and how would he handle drugs, women, and all of the other things that he would face having been raised in a small, religious orphanage. The young man said, "That will not happen. I want to go to medical school and when I finish, I will return here and help her in the orphanage." The last I heard, he had gone to the University in Juarez and completed school. He is now a Doctor of Veterinary Medicine practicing in Juarez and is still living in the orphanage.

As a result of the fame this young man achieved through soccer, a local businessman came to Josefina and paid for a building on the back part of the property. It is a complete physical education building. The kids can play soccer, basketball, and many games indoors.

The last time I talked to Josefina, she had over 100 children at the home; three were attending the Bible College we helped build, another four were attending the University in Juarez.

Josefina had started working with a young man whom she called her nephew. I doubt there was any blood relation, but she called him her nephew. Cruz Velasquez felt the call to go to the mountains and start working with the Tarahumara Indians to bring the gospel to them. Over the years, his ministry has grown and there are now several Tarahumara Indian pastors. They even have a small Bible school for future pastors.

Sometime in 2011, the National Church in Mexico City approached Cruz and asked him to take over the operations for the country of Mexico of home missions as a result of his success with the Tarahumara Indians. When he first started, Cruz lived in his pickup truck. He had nowhere else to live.

The last I heard, he had declined saying he felt his work with the Indians was not completed as he felt it should be.

One New Year's day after we had built the first building, a young girl, about 17 years of age, walked into the kitchen, laid a small bundle on the counter, and said, "This is my baby. She was born yesterday. I have no way of caring for her; give her a home." She then walked out the door. To my knowledge, no one knows where she went.

It is not unusual for the police to find a small child on a street and bring the child to Josefina. Many of the children did not know their names.

***

At the time we were working in Mexico, we met a Hermano Padilla. His dream was to build an elementary school in his area. The government stated all children would receive a 6th grade education. There were no schools in his area. The nearby barrio had a school, but the government did not have a teacher for lack of funds.

Hermano Padilla wanted to build a school with a Christian background. We started construction. He had some unusual requests. First, in addition to the school, he wanted a fence around the school. We poured a footing and then four rows of concrete blocks. We then set steel poles inserted into the blocks, and we put chain link fence put around. We then out concertina barbed wire around the top. The whole area looked like a prison. The mothers were elated. They lived in pallet homes with dirt floors. Poverty was everywhere but when they took their children to school, they felt they would be safe from kidnapping or stolen children.

The school grew and a great many children received a basic education. Eventually, a kitchen was added for free meals, computers were given to the school, and things were going well.

The drug wars started to spill over into this area. One night in the fall of 2011, someone drove a truck into the wall of the building. Someone broke in and stole the computers, the food, and the kitchen equipment. Hermano Padilla's son was called. He went to the school. Someone started firing at him with an AK47. So far as I know no one has been caught.

At about the same time, someone broke into an orphanage about two miles away, herded the children into a room, and shot and killed the ladies working there. We did not build that orphanage.

***

We met an interesting man named Maurion. He and his wife were from a substantial family. Both were educated teachers. They became strong Christians and felt they should start a school in an underprivileged area.

They went to a slum, actually the garbage dump south of the city of Juarez. They retrieved some thrown away large Coca-Cola signs and started a class. In this area, people lived in the city dump. They had an agreement: if someone threw some trash where you had your hut, you had first right to pick over whatever you wanted. It was not unusual to see a fire breakout from trash combustion.

Wes Kelly, the construction missionary we worked with, took a team in and built a small school along with dormitory space for the children. Many parents brought their children there as they could not feed them. Soon, the building was filled to capacity. Maurion's parents and his wife's parents objected to their activity; they felt they were working beneath their social status.

An American lady was taken to the school and made a comment to Maurion: "How can you do any good here? Look at the broken glass all around here. Look at the plastic bags being blown everywhere. His reply, "Yes, but I see flowers growing in the future.

Where you see broken glass, I see young people getting jobs and getting out of the slums where you see trash bags. It is all on what you choose to see in the future."

I could not stop being amazed at what he and his were doing. They merely felt they were doing what God had instructed them to do with their background as educators and administrators.

***

Lois and I were involved over several years in building churches and church-related buildings in Mexico.

It started when a retired engineer came by the church we were attending asking for volunteers to go to Juarez, Mexico to assist in the building of a Bible School for training of ministers in that country.

We volunteered to go. It was an interesting experience and an enjoyable one, although we worked hard as general labor and Lois worked in the kitchen. We went for one week and returned home.

The next summer, they were going to have a dedication of the building. I was the Mission's Deacon on our church board. The pastor could not go, so I was asked to go to represent our Church. When I arrived, I was greatly disappointed. The classrooms were far from complete. There were to be two apartments for teachers to live in on the grounds; none were completed, and the buildings were virtually unusable. When I returned and reported to the Church board, I stated if we were not able to give the school a useable project, we were not doing anyone a favor as the school could not afford to buy the material and hire the work done. The Church board voted to put together a crew from our local church as there were many men who were professional construction people who could finish the project, and they voted to put me in charge as I was the mission's Deacon. I agreed so long as we would get the necessary finances and I would have competent construction people in charge of the actual work.

I would make contact as well as get living accommodations and food and material ready so when our people arrived there would be no lost time and they could go to work immediately.

We scheduled the first trip in late February and opened it up, also, to high school upper-class students who wanted to go. I wanted the young people to get an experience of a different culture and language. The trip worked out to exceed our expectations. We were able to finish the structure and build some desks and other items the school needed. This was the beginning of a long relationship with the church in north Mexico.

I would go to Mexico, meet with the church leaders, and pick out a site that I felt our crew could finish in the allotted time and one the church leaders felt was most needed.

We were fortunate in that a man named Wes Kelley showed up. Wes had owned and operated a construction company in Carlsbad, New Mexico. He sold his business and became a full-time construction missionary. He became a valuable asset to us.

Wes and I would agree on a site. He would arrange for the footings to be poured. When our people arrived, the footings would be ready to go and we could start construction immediately. The average building was ten meters by twenty meters. This translates to 32.5 feet by 65 feet small concrete buildings with sheet metal roofs. Over the years, we helped Wes acquire the necessary cement mixers, welding torches, and equipment. Our people were professional carpenters, welders, electricians, etc. We were able to lay the blocks, weld trusses in place, install wiring, and complete the buildings in two weeks. This required long hours. Our ladies did the cooking and a lot of coordination.

Our people did an exceptional job and built quality buildings.

I will now try to tell of some of the unusual situations we ran into on the jobs.

On one church, one of our men was a professional engineer.

He felt since we were building a church, a steeple and cross should be on top of the building. He constructed the steeple and made a cross out of 4x4 wood painted in white. We mounted the steeple and cross on the church. The local pastor saw it and was horrified. At that point, we learned most were Protestant and churches in Mexico wanted nothing to do with crosses or any symbol of a church on the building. Mexico is a predominantly Catholic country, and the Catholic Church is strong on symbolism: the Stations of the Cross, statues of Jesus, and statues of our Lady of Guadalupe, their version of Mary the mother of Jesus. Therefore, Protestant churches abstained from any symbols to show a difference from the Catholic Church. After a long and heated discussion, because the cross and steeple were already in place, someone pointed out to the pastor that possibly someone would come to the church because of the cross and would be converted once they were exposed to the gospel. Reluctantly, the pastor agreed. Later, we learned that when we left, he got a 4x8 sheet of plywood, hand-painted a sign with the church's name on it, and nailed the plywood to the cross, thereby hiding the cross and seeing the church name painted on top of the church. This did not last too long as a strong gust of wind came along and the sheet of plywood snapped the cross off. There is now a small steeple and no cross on top of this church.

***

We were in a small village and helped build a Sunday school building. The church was adobe. An elderly widow of very limited means had no place to live. The church members built a small adobe building attached to the wall of the church and knocked a hole in the lower part of the wall of the church. When church serves were being held, the lady would get down on her knees and crawl through the hole, and she was at church.

***

We met a pastor in a small village. His house had no plumbing. His wife wanted a bathtub. The pastor made a bathtub out of concrete and put it in his backyard. He then constructed a wood frame and covered the wood frame with cardboard. He built into the frame a small wood-fired water heater. This was a small cylinder. He would pour water in the top, put wood in the base of the firebox, and his wife would have hot water when she took a bath in her cement tub. This worked well until some hot embers fell from the fire box and caught the cardboard exterior on fire. We then had a wife scrambling to get out of the tub.

***

One of the most memorable experiences was in the city of Lerdo, a suburb of Torreron. We were building a two-story cement block building to house a school. The building was 80 feet by 20 feet. We had completed the first floor, put in the rebars and bracing, and were ready to pour the concrete on the second floor so we could lay blocks and finish the building. I was trying to find a ready mix company with pumpers so we could pour the second floor. The pastor, Ramon Puentes, came to me with a suggestion. He stated a pumper and ready mix was expensive. He had an idea that would save us a lot of money. He knew a man who had a crew that would pour the concrete for us at a greatly lower cost. I met the crew chief. He assured me they could get the job done in less than a day. The agreement was we would have our two cement mixers mix the cement and pour the cement on the pavement. Our people would shovel the cement into five gallon buckets. His men would then carry the cement up to the 2nd floor and pour it where our men directed. The savings were considerable, and we agreed to the agreement. The big day arrived. The crew chief was a very small elderly man. He had fifteen men in his crew. We started the mixers. His crew gathered around him. They smoked some marijuana, passed a bottle of Tequila around a few times, picked up some empty cement sacks, and rolled them into a flat cover for their heads. The old man blew his whistle. They placed two stepladders by each other. The men would pick up a five gallon bucket full of cement, place it on his head, and walk up the ladder on the right. He would dump the cement where directed and walk down the ladder on the left. If they were getting behind our cement finishers, he would blow his whistle once and the men picked up the pace. If they were getting ahead of us, he would blow his whistle twice and they would slow down their pace. If I had not seen it, I would not have believed it. We had the entire floor poured at 4" thickness completed by 4:00 p.m. I paid the crew chief $250, how much he paid his men I do not know. The entire operation was done quickly and smoothly at a considerable savings of our money.

That building is now used as a Bible School to train ministers in that area.

***

During our trips to Mexico, we discovered many churches in small rural villages had no training or programs for the young children.

After many discussions, Mike Dollard, who was the children's pastor where we attended church and who was quite an expert on making and using puppets to get his point across, went to Mexico to several small villages to institute such a youth program. A friend of mine, John McCoy, designed a small puppet stage that could be made out of 2" plastic pipe and elbows. The stage could be assembled in a short time and packed up for reuse quickly. While Mike was talking to the church members on the use of puppets and how to make them, I would be outside cutting the pipes and making the kits. It was amazing to see the enthusiasm of the church workers and the excitement on the children's faces as they watched the puppets and heard stories of the Bible.

Here are some of the examples:

We went into this small village. The original church was a very small concrete building. The church had outgrown the building. A new church had been partially built. The original building was inside the new building. They were using it temporarily as a kitchen when they had church meals together. The new building had walls up, doors, windows, and a roof but the building had not been closed in on either end. The eaves had not been installed. As a result, birds would fly in and around during church services. The church was on a corner lot. The pastor's house was around the corner facing the side street. A small alley separated the pastor's home and the new church. While Mike was inside delivering his program, I was outside behind the building cutting the pipe and making the puppet kits. At lunchtime, Mike came to me and said, "There is quite a stinking odor upon that podium." I told him to come outside where I was working. The pastor had a few pigs he was raising for meat. He decided to build a pig pen. He used the back wall of the church as one wall for his pig pen and built the three other walls. He had a four wall enclosure. I was working next to the pig pen when making my kits while Mike was on the other side of the wall. The pig pen was directly behind the pulpit.

***

In another village, it was lunch time. The Mexican brothers took us to a store. We purchased some butter and several cans of soda. We stopped by a cornfield and picked some corn off the stalks. We went to a dry sandy river bed and built a fire. We threw the corn into the fire. When they decided the corn had roasted enough, they pulled the corn out, put butter on the hot corn, gave us a bottle of soda, and we had lunch. The corn was really very good. After the meal, our Mexican brothers picked out a nice shady spot, put their hats over their faces, and promptly had a siesta. Our interpreter told Mike and me, "The sand is clean, come and join us." Mike and I had our first outdoor siesta.

***

We were in the village of Saintiago-Papasquierro holding our seminar when we saw some local men putting plaster on an adobe wall. As the plaster dried, a form started taking shape on the wall. The workmen had not intentionally put any specific form on the wall; it was merely a job to them. The next morning, a figure or a silhouette was definitely on the wall. It was generally in the form of a human being. I did not see any defining features but the locals, in their minds, definitely did. Some felt it was a figure of Jesus; others felt it was the mother of Christ, the lady of Guadalupe. At any rate, by the time we quit work for the day many people had made a pilgrimage to it. There were flowers. Some small crosses had been placed in the ground. It had become overnight a small religious site for the people in that neighborhood.

***

Wes Kelley, the construction missionary we worked with, told me the following story. I did not see it.

West, at the time, had his own twin engine airplane and he agreed to take a missionary to a remote village to meet with some people about starting a church in this very remote isolated village. He stated the missionary was a large man, some 6'5" and about 230 pounds. They met the local people and were invited to eat with them in their home. The home was adobe with a dirt floor. The housewife was quite excited about having the two ministers come to their home and had cleaned her house very thoroughly. As they were eating, Wes noted the missionary seemed to be getting shorter.

The wife had sprinkled water on the floor to cut down on the dust and had sprinkled too much. The missionary's chair was sinking in the floor. The children were laughing; they thought it was funny. The wife was greatly embarrassed. Wes said they tried to assure the wife her efforts were greatly appreciated.

***

I was very surprised to see a very large Mennonite community in the central part of Mexico. It seems when many Mennonite people left Germany some went to the United States, some went to Canada, and a large group went to Mexico. They had acquired land and started building farms. At the time I was there in this one section, they produced about 25% of the apples produced in the country of Mexico. It was interesting. Their farms were large, the buildings were neat, and they used the latest in tractors and equipment but when they had to go to town, they used a horse and buggy in town. The Mexican government were appreciative of the fact that these were very industrious taxpaying citizens and made an agreement with them to keep lower taxes to lure more of them to Mexico. At the time we were there, some Canadian Mennonites were moving to Mexico for the cheaper land and lower taxes.

The men wore the black overalls, white shirts, and the traditional flat brimmed white straw hats. Mike and I were walking down the street and a young, good looking, blond-haired Mennonite man spoke to us in English with a slight Canadian accent. His wife was with him. She wore the traditional dress, German style, with a large bonnet on her head with a long visor. The entire time her husband was talking to us, she had the visor pulled over her face and was looking away from us. It was not proper for an outsider to look on the face of a Mennonite woman.

***

On one of our projects, I got a splinter in one of my fingers. I asked one of our Mexican friends if he had a Band-Aid. Much to my surprise, he went to the pharmacy and brought me one. That evening, I went to buy some and the clerk wanted to know how many I wanted. They sold them by the Band-Aid, not by the box. Later, I mentioned to Wes Kelley I was surprised they were sold by amount rather than the box. Wes replied, "You should ask for a cigarette; they would have sold you one."

The Tarahumara Indians

The Tarahumara Indian tribe in northern Mexico are an interesting people. They will tell you the Spanish are the sons of Satan and the Mexican is his first cousin. They did not fare too well under Spanish rule.

They are tremendous runners. Every October, they have a 200 mile foot race. Their footwear is quite interesting. They will find a tire that has been thrown away and trace the outline of their foot on the tread. Then, they will cut it out and drill some holes: one hole where a leather thong will be between the large toes of the foot and two holes along the side of the ankle. They will put leather thongs through the holes, tie them together on the ankle, and you are ready to go.

A village may consist of ten or more families. A village leader will get together with another village leader and they will decide to have a festival. Naturally, a foot race is the high point of the festival. The two leaders will meet, agree on a spot to have the race (say a race course is six kilometres, 30 laps is enough), and they will agree on the day. The night before the race, the medicine man of each village will walk over the course and sprinkle lotions and say a few prayers to give the other enemy team shin splints or something so they will lose the race. Naturally, the other team's medicine man will do the same. The rules of the race are quite simple. Each team will start to run. They will run until one side has a winner or until all have dropped out.

While the men are running, the women are busy making a corn beer called Tisquino. It is important to have bets placed before the race; it could be a dog, a chicken, anything to bet, but you will bet.

When there is a winner, all bets are paid off. They will have a feast and every man, woman, and child will drink lots of the homemade beer. They will pretty well drink until all are passed out. The next day, as they sober up, the visiting people will pack up and go home.

In recent years, you can see the women in town holding out their hands, but they are not begging. In their lore, the Great Spirit made the Tarahumara and that was good. He then made the white man and that was bad. If it wasn't for their prayers and incantation, the whole world would be destroyed; therefore, you owe the ladies a donation because if it wasn't for their beliefs you wouldn't even be here.

Their running ability caught the attention of some outsiders, and a group was taken to Colorado where an endurance race is held each year. The men were provided with new Nike shoes. The Indians fared badly. Their feet hurt so badly, and they were not familiar with the flashlights they were given. They ran holding the lights up and could not see. The next year, they used the flashlights properly as they started running in the dark, and they wore their sandals they were used to. The Tarahumara's came in first through tenth, and the tenth was a forty-five-year-old man.

Physically, they are not large people; rather short. The women appear to be rather on the heavy side until you realize she is literally wearing all of her clothes she owns. She may be wearing seven or eight skirts. If she wants to stop and let a baby nurse and take a nap, she will take one skirt off and wrap the baby in it to keep it warm while sleeping. She will take another skirt off and make a pillow of it as she rolls it up. She will take another off and put it across her chest while she is sleeping, so there are some practical uses.

The men wear a loin cloth-type of garment and when they sit down, they will reach down and pull the tail of the garment up and tuck it into their waistband.

I paid a Tarahumara lady to make Lois a ceremonial dress and hat. I brought it home. Lois said the hand stitching was extremely good. I could not get her to wear the outfit; she ultimately gave it away.

Ailee Kenboom

Ailee Kenboom is an interesting man. He is a member of the Mossi tribe of Burkina Faso, West Africa. He is the first son by the first wife; this makes him special in the family social order. When he was about 6 to 8 years old, his father decided he should get an education as he was the first son. The family lived in the bush near Koudogou. His father took him to a Christian Missionary school near Ouadaougodoo and said, "This is my son; give him an education." With that, he went back home. When the school year ended, Ailee walked the 40 kilometres back home. When he felt it was time for the next school year to start, he came back. Ailee proved himself to be a very intelligent young man and wanted to improve himself. He completed all of the schooling the missionaries could give him. By this time, he was a Christian even though his family were Animists. The Church leaders felt Ailee had good leadership potential and sent him to England where he received his BA. He then enrolled at the Assembly of God Theological Seminary in Springfield, Missouri. Ailee told me, "You Americans are statistically oriented. When I was registering, the young lady wanted to know how old I was. I replied, 'I have no idea.' She stated, 'You must know when you were born.'" He said, "Young lady, in my country, in my tribe, in my culture, age never comes up. In, the evening, the family will sit around a fire and then one of the elders will say, 'You Ailee, are the son of so and so, who is your father,' etc. I must repeat it so I am accurate and can pass it onto my sons. It never comes up but if I were to ask when was I born, I would be told you were born at the time of planting or during the rainy season or time of harvest. But if it is important, you pick out a date and that is what I will use." This is out of the Old Testament – Oral Tradition.

He returned to Burkina Faso. When we visited him, he was pastor to a large church in the city. This was interesting. Burkina Faso was a French colony; therefore, the official and written language is French. The same church building houses two separate congregations: one a local native language and then Ailee pastors the official French-speaking congregation.

One Sunday morning, Ailee took us to a small mission church he had started. There may have been 30 people in attendance. Since we were the white guests, we had to sit up front facing the congregation. The musical group was fascinating. One young man was playing what is called tom-toms. A young boy of about 14 was sitting on the frame of what looked to be a square frame of 1 x 10 boards. A goat skin had been stretched across the frame, and he pounded on the skin. A young lady had a bowl. It appeared to be the bowl part of a large gourd that had been cut in half. It had a network of beads and shells woven into it, dangling from the outside of the bowl. She would toss the bowl in the air and catch it. When she did, the beadwork made a clicking sound. She would also shake it for a different sound. A middle-aged man sitting next to me had a piece of angle iron about 16 inches in length with a small metal rod. He would hit the angle iron from different angles, making various sounds. I did not know the language, but I found it interesting. They all started and stopped in time and kept a nice rhythmic beat to it.

Ailee invited us to his home for dinner. The home was a mixture of adobe and cement. It was three rooms. On the wall were a couple of bookcases filled with books. Also on the wall were his various degrees: a BS, a Masters of Divinity, and a PhD. The building had a dirt floor. What was most surprising was his two teenaged sons came in wearing Ozzie Smith T-shirts, the former St. Louis Cardinals' baseball player. Kerosene lamps hung from the ceiling from hooks in the ceiling.

John Weidman

I first met John Weidman when we went to the West African country of Togo.

John's father was a missionary to West Africa. He took John to Africa when John was 4 years old. When I met him, he was 56 and had only lived in the United States ten years and that was to go to college, go to seminary, and go on furlough from the mission fields. He was much more familiar with Africa than he was America. He stated his older brother died of black water fever and was buried in the white section in Burkina Paso Cemetery in Ouadaudougou. I have mentioned Ailee Kenboom who is pastoring a large church. John's father arranged the purchase of the church property.

There is a large tree on the lot. It had been used as a judgment tree. When someone would bring charges against someone, the chiefs would sit under the tree and render judgment. On some occasions, a person was hanged from that tree. John stated the Africans in many ways were very superstitious about death and the hangings. They felt the evil spirits were in that tree. When John's father approached the chiefs about buying the property, the chiefs agreed. John stated his father wrote to the church headquarters about the agreement to get this choice property and were thrilled. The chiefs had a different idea. They felt since there were so many evil spirits in the tree, they would ultimately chase the white man out and they could get the property back for free and continue to use it as a judgment tree. Obviously, the chiefs were wrong as it is a very large thriving church now.

We arrived the latter part of January. John stated about three weeks before we got there, there had been an attempted coup. The dictator of neighboring Ghana, Jerry Rawlings, did not like the dictator of Togo. He permitted some rebels to train and provided them with arms, with the idea to overthrow the leader of Togo. The two neighboring countries are like going from St. Louis city into St. Louis County: an imaginary line. Ghana was an English colony; therefore, the official document language is English. Togo had been a French colony; therefore, the official documents are French. There are families on both countries that cannot visit without getting visas and passports. On the border is the West African School of Advanced Theology. On the big day, the student body arose and started to go to the dining hall when they were suddenly alarmed. The rebels were starting the revolution in the courtyard of the school. John stated he was in his office downtown when bullets started coming through the windows. He was on the floor under his desk when the phone rang. John answered it. It was the dean of the seminary stating they were under attack and asking what should he do. John said, "I told him to hide under his desk and pray, that is what I'm doing." The battle only lasted for a couple of days. Most of the rebels were killed, their bodies thrown into a dump truck and hauled away. John told us this had happened two weeks before our arrival. That did not make me feel any too safe while I was in Togo.

***

John was a large help to us getting our visas, money changed, etc. When I got in his car, I noticed several containers of water and rolls of toilet paper. I inquired about the need. John stated that was for his African friends. He said if they had to go, they had to go now; there was no time for niceties. I asked was this diet, heredity, what caused this? John's answer was very practical and to the point. He said, "No, it is for the convenience of the mothers." He asked since I had been in Africa had I seen mothers with babies on their backs. I replied many ladies had babies wrapped onto their backs. John stated that is the problem. Babies are human beings and have bodily functions. The mothers did not mind a little moisture on their backs, but they did not want feces. He told me each morning, first thing, they gave the baby an enema; the child cannot have a bowel movement. As a result, as infants, they do not have bowel movements and develop muscle control of their bowels. Therefore, as they mature, they will spend the rest of their lives with a sort of diarrhea. But he said since many of the girls were getting educated, they were now using syringes. Stupidly, I asked, "What did they do before?" John smiled, as gotcha, and used a local term, which merely meant the mothers would give a child using an oral enema. I said, "You've got to be kidding!" He stated, "No. It was going on for centuries before."

On the capital building in Lome, Togo there are signs on the walls of the building: "DO NOT URINATE HERE."

***

John and another missionary took us out to visit a small Bible school in the bush, and they took us to a spot where someone the night before had sacrificed an animal and made a burnt offering to their god. It felt strange to actually see the remains of the animal and fire pit and ashes that were still warm.

***

John told us of an incident. He said, "I am white, I am a missionary. There are not too many of us here. There is a Catholic priest; he, too, is white; he too is an American. That makes us compatriots in many ways." The priest and John had become good friends. They played cards, played tennis, etc. John said, "We all make mistakes and most of the time the priest got the better of me, but one time the priest did something that John would not let him forget.

The priest lived in his quarters and obviously was single. In Africa it is quite hot. John stated the priest slept in his quarters in the nude; no one else was around. The priest went to Brussels, Belgium to participate in a conference on starvation, food distribution, and many other topics pertaining to West Africa. While in Brussels, the he had access to food and drink not available in Togo. He had dinner, a couple of drinks, and went to his room to go to bed. In the middle of the night, he felt the urge to go to the bathroom. As was his habit, he was nude. He did not turn a light on. He took two steps, opened the door, and stepped through like he was in his quarters back at home. He had forgotten he was in a hotel in Brussels. As soon as he stepped through the door, he realized his error. He was in the corridor in the hotel. He turned around, and the door shut behind him. Panic stricken, he spotted a newspaper someone had discarded in a waste can. He quickly retrieved the paper and had a form of cover. He then relieved himself in a waste basket and down the hall saw a phone. The priest called the front desk, explaining he had a small problem. The voice on the phone said, "Yes, we know. We've been watching you on the monitor." John stated he could never pull one off like that.

***

John told us they felt they could get some movies, set up out in the desert, and show films about Christ as a way of reaching some natives. It is amazing: you can go through the desert and see no one. Stop your car, and it seems as if the people pop up from the sand. He said it was not unusual to get to an area early in the day, set up a screen, and get things ready to go when the darkness arrives, and people will show up: several hundred. They soon found out movies would not work as the people could not comprehend a figure on the screen and the talking. They then changed tactics and set it up as a slide show. They would show a picture and explain the meanings. This was working until they showed Jesus entering Jerusalem on a donkey. They lost the crown completely. Everyone knows that if Jesus was truly a big shot, he would be riding a camel.

***

John took us to his home and introduced us to his wife Betty. She was truly a gracious lady and had prepared a delicious home-cooked meal for us. I felt like a king. In retrospect, I have great admiration for the wives of the missionaries. If the missionary is gone, the natives expect the wife to step in. Betty had gone to the market. She had boiled the water to make it safe, then washed the water in a lye solution, rinsed it off, and rinsed the water in an iodine solution before she felt it was safe to use. I find it hard to image doing that for literally every meal you eat.

***

One day, John Weidman took us to a place in Lome, Togo. It was a quiet area. There was an area with trees and flowers, and it looked quite nice. John stated this was the center of the black magic religion. At the corner, there was a small open shed with a roof on it. In the center, there was a form of a man from the waist up. It had the shape of a human being with no facial features. There were a couple of capes of cloth and some of straw that had been placed on it. There were some bowls of water and fresh fruit on the ground in front of it. Millions of people across the world worshipped that form.

John did not enter the shed; instead he started to enter the ground around the shed. A man came running out, quite excited. He was yelling something. He and John got in quite an animated conversation. After a bit, John came over and stated we should move on. I asked him what the reason for the excitement was. The man told John we could not go in as that was a holy place. If he let us in, something bad would happen to us as the gods would not like it. John told him he did not believe in their gods; therefore, nothing would happen to us. The man replied if he let us go in, something bad would happen to him. He was not going to let us in. John told us it wasn't worth us getting involved in a big affair as we were visitors, and we left.

He then took us about a block away where we saw the Fetische Marchette, the fetish market. It was about a city block in size. There were all kinds of staples, dried frogs, lions' claws, and weird things I could not describe. Basically, if one went to a witch doctor with a petition, the witch doctor would tell you to get a dead frog, grind it up, and ingest it; your petitions would be answered. One man came up to me and tried to sell me a small stone that had a hole in it. If I would buy the stone, I would need to boil it in water and pour the water over my head. Headaches would be cured forever. I felt filthy walking around such a place.

***

John told us he was raised in Africa, but he felt he had a normal childhood. When his parents and a couple of other missionaries started to build a compound for a Bible School, the living quarters area had a lot of lions in the area. A couple of times, the lions tried to chew the tires off the trucks and cars. The missionaries dug a large hole. They placed and set bait in it. They captured and killed eight lions using this method.

***

John told us after his brother died of black water fever, his parents took all measures they could to protect him. His father constructed a box. John described it as a large bread box. His mattress and covers were put in. When John was put in his bed, his father would put him in the box and then tack screen wire across the top and sides to keep insects from biting him. His parents slept with screen netting around their bed.

***

He told us his father built an adobe home for them to live in. His mother said she would live in a mud home but she would not have a dirt floor. John's father poured a cement floor. John stated a man would come by and sell wood to his father so his mother could have a fire to cook on. One day his father was joking and he told the wood seller, "I buy wood from you, you never bring me anything." A few days later around dusk, there was a clapping outside the door. One did not knock because if you knocked, and the termites had eaten your door away, you would have to replace the door. If you clapped and the owner of the house opened the door and it collapsed, it was their problem. John's father opened the door, and it was the wood seller. He told John's father, "I bring you this large constrictor snake, much good meat." The man dragged a large snake into the house. It was about 15 feet in length. His father asked if the snake was dead. The man replied, "Yes. I hit him in the head with a club." About this time, the snake opened its eyes and started to move around. The wood seller screamed and ran out the door. John said, "We now had a large snake in the house." This snake started toward the kitchen. He apparently smelled the food. John's father attempted to grab him by the tail and pull him out. The snake was in no mood and turned his head around and started after John's father. His mother got up on a chair and was screaming. His father ran into the bedroom with the snake chasing him. When he came out, he had a shotgun in his hands. As the snake came out of the bedroom, his father shot the snake, blowing the head off. He dragged the carcass out of the house. Then his parents started cleaning the mess up on the floor. After they cleaned up, his father went out with his machete to cut the meat up so it could be used, but there was nothing left. As soon as the snake was dragged outside, the neighbors came out with their machetes and took it all away. The Weidman family did not get any meat from the snake.

I told John that I did not consider that as being a normal childhood…

Africa

Lois and I went to East Africa on a photographic safari. We had spent several days in Kenya on the Masi-Mara game preserve. We then departed Kenya and entered Tanzania. We left Dars-EsSaloom, the capital, to go to the NeoNgo crater. We were told it is the 8th wonder of the world. It is truly something to see. Many years ago, a volcanic eruption occurred. Instead of an overflow of lava, the entire mountain top collapsed, forming this huge crater. The mountains around the crater are from 8,000 to 9,000 feet in altitude. It covers more than four hundred square miles. It is very unusual in that it has a mini ecosystem. Virtually all of the animals in Africa live on the floor of the canyon. The lodges are located on the rim over the canyon. The one we stayed at was roughly like a Boy Scout camp. The cabins had cots for beds. Electrical power was from dark to 10:00 p.m. They then turned the power off. If one had to get up in the middle of the night, you needed a candle or flashlight.

To get to the floor of the canyon was an interesting experience: a rather precarious ride on a Jeep-type four-wheel vehicle down the face of the cliff.

One evening, as Lois and I were walking from the dining hall to our cabin, Lois leaned against me saying, "Jack, I think I am going to faint," and then she passed out. It was just getting dark. I picked Lois up and carried her to the first cabin. I saw light coming from underneath the door. I knocked on the door and a lady named Helen Wilson from London, England was kind enough to let me bring Lois in and put her on a cot. Miss Wilson got a wet cloth and wiped her brow and loosened the neck on her shirt and after a few minutes, Lois started to regain consciousness. Miss Wilson suggested I get our stuff and she would pack and we would swap cabins, which I thankfully did. I went to what passed for an office and was informed we were out in bush country where there were no medical facilities anywhere. If Lois was still sick in the morning, they would get on a shortwave radio and have a doctor come out from Nairobi, Kenya – 300 miles away by piper cub. Lois had asked if I could get some extra covers as she was chilled. They gave me a mildewed blanket.

When I put Lois to bed, she would not let me take her shoes off. She was chilled and wanted to keep as much clothing on her as possible. During the night, I heard Lois say, "Jack, I need your help." I got out of bed, grabbed my flashlight, lit a candle, and asked what I could do to help. During the day, Lois had purchased an open-ended wooden bracelet and put it on her wrist. During the night, tossing and turning, she had hooked the bracelet to the buttonhole on her opposite sleeve bush jacket and had handcuffed herself. Needless to say, it was with great relief I performed the necessary surgery on her jacket and saved her at 3:00 a.m.

The next day, we left the high mountain country and went to a place called Lake Manyara. This was truly a beautiful place. The compound overlooked the lake. The lake was literally covered with pink flamingo birds. You could hardly see the water for the birds. The area was literally teeming with wild game. In one tree, there were seven lions sprawled out sleeping up in the tree. The weather was perfect, and Lois started to recover from her episode. After a couple of days, she started feeling better and we decided to go for a walk. We left the fenced-in compound to wander down a little dirt path. The country was beautiful, the weather was perfect, and Lois was getting her strength back. Suddenly on our left, from the heavy bush, came a whole pack of baboons. There were baboons in front of us, behind us, and all around us. Lois whispered to me, "What do we do?" I replied, "We've done it. Just stand still and make no sudden moves and be perfectly quiet. Maybe they will go away." As we stood there, a couple of them glanced at us, but they kept going and disappeared into the bush on our right. We decided we had walked far enough and went back to the compound. I was surprised on how large some of them were. Up close and personal, they are much bigger than I had seen them in the zoo.

***

I was in the West African country of Ghana, the capitol city of Accra. I was talking to my friend, Kweiku Obeng. I asked him, "How many kids are in your family?"

He replied, "I do not understand the meaning of your question."

I stated, "I'm sorry. I am an American, and I think as an American. I did not mean any offense. Let me rephrase the question. How many brothers and sisters do you have?" He replied, "I have no idea." When he saw the surprised look on my face, he stated, "Let me explain."

"In this part of West Africa, there are three religions:"

1. "Christianity. If one is a Christian, one has one wife. A person can be Baptist, Methodist, Lutheran, Catholic, or whatever. If Christ is the focal point of the religion, they are called a Christian. That is the smallest religion in this part of West Africa. If one is a Christian, one has one wife. I am a Christian; I have one wife. When I became a Christian, I was expelled from my tribe. As I said, Christianity is the smallest of all religions in this part of Africa."

2. "Muslim. If one is a Muslim, one can have four wives.

However, if one of his wives displeases him, he can, in front of two witnesses, tell her three times, 'I divorce you,' and he is rid of her. She has no recourse; possibly, she can return to her family if they will accept her; otherwise, she is on her own. Any children stay with the husband. A man can have several wives, but he cannot have more than four at any one time. This religion is small but larger than Christianity."

3. "Animanism. This is the blood of animals sacrifice offering poured over a fetish doll. In the past, humans were offered but no longer. This leads into Voodoo, Black Magic, and the ultimate: Juju. Make no mistake, this is a religion. This is the largest religion in this part of West Africa. My tribe is Animist. My father is Animist. If one is an Animist, one can have as many wives as one wants. I do not know how many wives my father has. He has at least ten, maybe more. Since I do not know how many wives he has, I do not know how many brothers and sisters I have."

I then asked, "What happens if a man has multiple wives and converts to Christianity, what happens to the wives?"

"He is told: do not take any more wives but since you

101

have made a commitment to the others, take care of them. This is the best compromise we can think of."

Egypt and Israel

Lois and I were in Cairo, Egypt. The museums and antiquities were something we really enjoyed. We decided to take a side trip to a place called Luxor. In ancient times, it was known as Thebes in the Bible. This is known as the Valley of the Kings because of the large number of pharaohs buried in the various mountains, King Tut among them. On the east side of the Nile River are the huge obelisks, temples pertaining to the sun god; it truly is amazing. On the west side of the river are the tombs.

When we arrived at the airport, a young man tried to sell me a hat because he said the sun on the west side would become very hot. I told him I did not need a hat. After several attempts, he came back with a fly whisk made from the hair of the tail of a horse and said it was very effective, I must have one. I told him I did not need nor want one. After he became convinced he could not sell me anything, he moved several feet away where he felt safe and yelled at me, "You one big tightwad!" Lois commented, "He knows you."

The trip was very informative and enjoyable from my point of view. When we went to the airport to return to Cairo, it became very interesting. For all intents, the small airport was closed at night. We could see the airplane sitting on the tarmac. The Egyptians had no idea how many tickets they had sold or how many people were trying to get on the plane. There was a rope stretched across access to the plane. Then they announced that whoever could run the fastest could get a seat and anyone left over would have to spend the night and not know when they could get back to Cairo. I told Lois, "I can run faster than you; I will try to get ahead and get on the plane and save you a seat." The rope was dropped, and the mob started the race. I am racing Germans, Italians, Japanese, and all kind of nationalities. Fortunately, I could still run and made it despite some rather pointed elbows thrown my way. Lois and I did make the flight back to Cairo.

When we left Cairo by bus to go to the Israeli border, it was about 7:00 a.m. When we arrived at the Suez Canal and took a rather hazardous ferry ride across, it was close to noon. While we were waiting for transportation into Israel, I noticed Lois and a group of women following a man in flowing Arab robes leaving and going over a sand dune. One of the ladies had communicated with the man that the ladies needed to find restroom facilities as we had been traveling for several hours with no break. The man led the women between some sand dunes where they could have some privacy. The women could dig a hole in the sand and take care of their business.

As he left, he told the ladies, "When you come back, walk in my footsteps only" as they had just gone through a mine field. One of the ladies, as she squatted down to do her business, sat down on a cactus. Then several ladies had to remove the portions of the cactus from the woman's rear.

As we left the Suez and crossed over the sand dunes, we were surprised to see all types of destroyed military equipment. We saw destroyed tanks, cannons, trucks, and all kinds of military equipment. That area had been a major battlefield between Egyptian and Israeli armies. The debris had just been left out in the desert. It was a sobering sight to see so much destruction of so much equipment.

When we arrived in Israel, the bus stopped at a restaurant. Before we got off the bus, a car pulled up and parked next to the bus. The car had a telephone symbol painted on the doors of the car. I assume it was a telephone company car. Two young men got out of the car. When they exited the car, they reached into the car and on the front of their seats between their legs each man had an Uzi submachine gun. They took the guns to the trunk. I saw each man had a container with full military uniforms and combat gear. They laid the Uzis on top of the military gear and went in to eat. I was later informed every Israeli citizen was in the military reserve ready to be activated to duty at any time.

This brought home to me the fact that these people live in

constant threat of war all the time as they are totally surrounded by enemies.

While in Israel, we saw so many things of historical and religious significance: Golgotha, the River Jordan, and one place that really stood out in my mind was the Temple Mount, The Dome of the Rock, and the Wailing Wall. To see many people praying there and putting their prayer requests in the cracks of the wall was amazing. It was a privilege to actually touch the wall. So much history, so much meaning of the wall; it was an emotional experience for me.

Moldova

I was privileged to go with a group of people to the small country of Moldova. This is a very small country between Romania and the Ukraine. This country had been part of the Soviet Union; therefore, it was dominated by the Russians for many years. The capital city of Chisinau has about 1.5 million people. It is the same latitude as Minneapolis and they have the same severe winters. At the time we were there, it was estimated there were over 100,000 children that had no families and were homeless. The government had some orphanages but nowhere near the amount needed. When a child became 17 years of age, they were told to move on. These young people had no skills. Many of the girls turned to prostitution as a way to survive. The economy was in shambles. The country had poor infrastructure. They had to buy all of their electrical power from Russia. All the buildings in town were heated with steam heat. The government turned the heat on November 1st and turned it off on March 31st. The hotel we stayed in had half of the lights in the lobby turned off in an effort to lower costs. I sent some laundry out and when it was returned, I discovered the hotel had farmed it out to local ladies who washed the clothes by hand. They were far from dry when they were returned to me. The elevators usually stopped two to three feet short of the floor. We had to climb out after we had pried the doors open.

A man from St. Charlies, Missouri had donated money to a local church to buy what had been a Soviet youth camp. The church was trying to convert the barrack buildings into single family homes. A Christian couple would move into the completed building with the understanding they would become foster parents to some of the many homeless children in an effort to provide a Christian family atmosphere to these young people.

We were assigned one of these buildings. I went to the local man in charge and motioned I needed a saw to cut a 4 foot x 8 foot piece of plywood as we were installing a subfloor. Since I did not speak the local language, we communicated by hand signs. Finally, he pointed to a two man hand saw. It would take a lot of time to use this and the accuracy of the cut would not be good. We had anticipated this would happen and brought some money along to buy some tools. One of our men went into the city with our interpreter. Out of a large city, he found one DeWalt skill saw. You could buy one in the United States for about $80. He had to pay $300 United States dollars for the saw. Our interpreter came to me and said, "I cannot believe you people paid $300 for that saw…" I stated we were on limited time, and the saw would help us work faster as well as be more accurate and besides, we were going to leave the saw with them. He replied, "I could hire five men to work for a full month at nine hours a day for that much money." If I drove a nail in and it bent, I would pull it out and throw it away. They would grab it like it was gold, straighten it out, and use it again.

Their brooms were branches cut off of trees and tied together. They swept with them.

I had read of the persecution of Christians by Soviet governments. I actually met some people that had been imprisoned. Their crime: they had a Bible. If one owned a Bible, it became a very precious item. These people came up with an ingenious way of printing their own Bible. The washing machines were the old-fashioned ones with ringers at the top. These believers had actually made the ringers into printing presses. If the secret police made a raid, it did not occur to them to confiscate the ringers of a washing machine.

To go to a church service was very enlightening. It was a privilege to openly worship God. These people were very emotional about that privilege. It was also somewhat of a cultural shock to receive the brotherly Christian kiss. A man would be grabbed and arms wrapped around your shoulders and given a kiss right on the lips by another man. Female and male members would shake hands. People of the same sex would get a rather large juicy kiss.

It was not uncommon for a farmer to have a horse and then plow by the horsepower. The standard of living was far below what I expected.

I also came away with a greater appreciation of the blessings I have had in my life, and it made me appreciate the opportunity of being a Christian and having freedom of expression.

Greece

Lois and I went on a historical tour of Greece. It was very interesting to me.

We were taken to the spot where legend tells was the spot where the Apostle Paul stood and gave his sermon to the Corinthians. Being a Christian, that had considerable significance to me.

We saw the space where the first Olympics were held.

We were taken to Thermopylae, the space where the 300 Spartans held out against such overwhelming odds until they were killed by a traitor informing the enemy of how to attack them.

While we were there, I saw a plaque about 100 yards away. During World War II, a small group of Australian and New Zealand soldiers were actually winning a battle against a much larger German force. The Germans flew in a brigade of German Paratroops before the small Aussie and Kiwis were defeated. I thought to myself, "Would man ever learn and live in peace?" Apparently not.

Ireland

Lois and I were in Dublin, Ireland. You cannot go to Ireland without visiting a pub. As we were enjoying our drink, a pleasant gentleman came over and sat down with us. Obviously with our dress, we were easily identified as Americans. The man introduced himself as John. Immediately, he asked what we thought of the troubles in Ireland. I was not about to get involved in Irish politics with a total stranger. I commented since I was a visitor, I only knew what I had read in the papers. He says, "Laddie, the troubles will not be over until we are one solid Ireland, one country, one government." I asked what about the people in the north, they were Protestant. They seemed to like the British form of government, schools, and their lifestyle. He responded, "Ah laddie, they don't belong here; send them all back to where they belong. They have only been here seven hundred years." I thought to myself, "How long do you have to live someplace to be accepted as a local?"

Germany

Munich, Germany has many beautiful and interesting places to visit.

There is a beautiful park named English Gardens. It is well-maintained. There are bandstands to hear concerts and walking lanes.

Lois and I had an interesting incident. There is one place in the park that is the designated nude sunbathing area. As we went through the park, there was one area where there were many nude people. There were handsome young men playing Frisbee, reading, or just sunbathing. There were beautiful young women, small children playing, and many elderly people just getting some sun in the nude. For Lois and me coming from a conservative place like St. Louis, Missouri, it was quite surprising.

Ironically, we were told the nude area was restricted. If one were to leave that area, they would be arrested for indecent exposure. Go figure.

While in Munich, we went to see Dachau. This was a concentration camp a few miles outside of Munich. During World War II, many people were imprisoned, tortured, and burned. The place has been cleaned up a great deal, but the ovens where people were cremated are still there as well as some of the original barracks. The effect of how humans could be so cruel is sobering.

After we returned home, I had the photos of Dachau developed. I received a call from Jeff Saunders, a friend of mine. His office was near mine. Jeff was president of an insurance company. Jeff invited me to lunch; I agreed. While we were eating lunch, I mentioned Lois and I had just returned from Germany and I had photos of Dachau. I asked him if he would be interested in seeing them. Jeff replied he had no interest in seeing anything concerning Dachau. He then told me his story.

Jeff said prior to World War II, he was an Oklahoma farm boy. He was drafted, fought in Africa, and then in Italy. His unit saw a great deal of action as they moved toward the Alps and Germany. He stated much of Europe was very beautiful and scenic. He would like to take his wife to that area but, emotionally, he felt he would not be able to take it.

By the time they came up the Alps to a place called Dachau, he was a hardened veteran. He told me he personally had shot and killed the SS Guard troops guarding the gate to Dachau with his Thompson submachine gun. He then shot the locks off the gates, and he was the first American soldier to enter Dachau. Jeff stated what he saw he could never forget. It was horrible. He had no desire to see my photos.

Lois and I were having dinner at the Hilton Hotel in Munich, Germany. The dining room was very crowded. A waiter was attempting to go between the table we were sitting at and a table directly behind me. Just as the waiter was behind me, a man at the table across from me arose from his chair. The man's shoulder hit the bottom of the waiter's elbow. The waiter had several steins of Lowenbrau beer on the tray. The shoulder caused the waiter to elevate his tray, resulting in me getting baptised with at least six steins of beer. The head waiter came over to me and said the hotel would pay for the cleaning. As I was on the elevator to go shower and change clothes, the looks I received from the other passengers on the elevator were somewhat amusing. When I went to check out from the hotel, they had a charge for the cleaning of the suit with a surcharged for expedited service. Needless to say, I was a little upset and the hotel graciously decided to forgo the charge for the cleaning.

Austria

Lois and I were in Vienna, Austria when the Soviet empire collapsed. We met some English speaking people who told us we could get a train into Budapest, Hungary with no problem. We decided we may never get to this part of the world again, so we would try to go. We checked out of our hotel in Vienna and bought train tickets to Budapest. On our way, about an hour out of Budapest, the train stopped. We were informed some Polish protesters had blocked the track as a result of a grievance in Poland. I could never figure out how a blocking of the tracks in Hungary would assist their problem in Poland. The train backed up and rerouted into Budapest. We found there are some beautiful buildings in Budapest. We checked into the Intercontinental Hotel. We were very fortunate. Our room had a very good view of the Danube River directly underneath our window. Just across the river were the ruins of an old Roman fort. The clerk at the desk told us that evening on the rooftop of the hotel there would be a performance of songs, music, and dance of the Hungarian folk dance as well as history. We booked ourselves in for dinner and the show. It was truly a beautiful show and an enjoyable evening.

On the streets, the ruins of the statutes of Stalin and Lenin were still on the streets where the Hungarian people had pulled them down. There were still Russian soldiers walking around the city. Vendors were selling parts of Russian uniforms.

It was an interesting time.

It so happened by accident this occurred on Lois' birthday. So on the morning of her birthday, I ordered breakfast in bed. I must brag on myself a little. I mentioned to Lois I had arranged this special occasion for her birthday: breakfast in bed, the old Roman fort across the river, and a beautiful view of the city. Like any good wife who wants to bring me down to earth, Lois looked at me, smiled, and said, "What are you going to do to top this next year?"

I replied, "I'm not even going to try."

Made in the USA
Monee, IL
04 June 2023

35240947R00070